TRASH

TRASH

The Graphic Genius of
Xploitation Movie Posters

BY JACQUES BOYREAU

CHRONICLE BOOKS

SAN FRANCISCO

Acknowledgments I wish there were more rube connoisseurs, Xploitation cheerleaders, and rogue intellects, but these are the people I can thank: Pat Fisher of Cine-Cyde; Little Vickki Vaden; Jack Stevenson; Joe McDonald; Rob Robertson; Greg Pierce from the Warhol; Will "Son of Bare Knuckles" Viharo; Ken Flagg; Dan Simpson; Robot Phil; Creepy James; CX; Olaf; Zubee; Steve Moore, Alan Rapp, Steve Mockus, Sara Schneider, and Beth Steiner at Chronicle Books; and most of all, Scott Moffett.

Library of Congress Cataloging-in-Publication Data:
Boyreau, Jacques.
Trash: the graphic genius of Xploitation movie posters
/ Jacques Boyreau.
p. cm.
ISBN: 0-8118-3417-4
1. Film posters, American 2. Exploitation films. I. Title.

PN1995.9.P5 B69 2002
791.43'75—dc21   2001047317

Manufactured in Singapore

Designed by Sara Schneider

Distributed in Canada by Raincoast Books
9050 Shaughnessy Street
Vancouver, British Columbia V6P 6E5

10 9 8 7 6 5 4 3

Chronicle Books LLC
85 Second Street
San Francisco, California 94105

www.chroniclebooks.com

CONTENTS

INTRODUCTION

Long past its pioneering years, glory years, and weird years, Hollywood Product today favors inbreeding and multiple anti-climax, becoming a feedback loop of let-downs. Grand survivor, regardless of who's boss, Hollywood knows where to pillage. It goes to Xploitation Cinema for goods.

Starting with the adoption of hit-and-run "saturation bookings" (proven effective throughout the '60s by the likes of trash mandarins Joseph E. Levine and American International Pictures), top-echelon Hollywood continues to mimic aspects of the shove-it-down-their-throats Xploitation genome. The results? A cobbling together of market blitz and elitist innuendo, the tease 'n' squeeze that can't quite please.

Back in an age of screwier pretensions and keener depravities, films such as *Gladiator, Eyes Wide Shut, Bring It On, Jurassic Park,* and *Hannibal* would have been designated by their Trash lineage. In other words, a hip student would line them up in their respective genres: Sword 'n' Sandal, Sin in the Suburbs, Horny Cheerleader, Giant Reptile Rampage, and Cannibal Gross-Out. Today, however, superficial copycatisms and total sleaze trips must be made amenable to high-end delusions. An accurate soul-search of Hollywood's *déclassé* genealogy cannot be undertaken by those intravenoused by studio public relations.

Fortunately, we have created this book: *Trash: The Graphic Genius of Xploitation Movie Posters.*

At the level of pure pleasure, our premise is simple: Look! *Trash*'s graphic zeal shows, in comparison to the "headshot" poster design of today, how a great commercial art form has palsied. Buried in art-by-committee gulags of market research and corporate niggling, the spirit of the sell and the integrity of schlock are hurting. Creative tag-lines, psychedelia, op-art, punk cut-and-paste, jazzy segmentation, cartoon intervention, color riots, and brazen minimalism have all been dumped. Movie poster ballsiness is, like, *snuffed.*

But let us penetrate a few years into the past, into the dark-sun realm of Xploitation. There are those of us, filmmaker and citizen alike, who have not forgotten. They tried to nail us with their dupe-guns, but they missed. Relax, buddy, help is on the way.

Shared voyeurism, after all, is the current between aesthetics and audiences. Our trawling trash-eye seeks Sex-and-Violence (which is like one word to me). Avoiding the Hollywood bootlick, *Trash* presents Smut and Convulsion . . . Glamour and Horror . . . Action and Madness.

So ponder *Trash.* Ponder obscure film companies like Rio Pinto, Fanfare, Aurora, Magna Pictures, Brigadier, Genie. Begin the mammoth count of big-studio excursions into Xploitation. Study the silk-screen beauty of posters like *Pretty Poison,* the spirographs of *Twisted Nerve,* the ropy mess of *Squirm.* Delve into the warped minutiae of the lobby card for *De Sade.* Realize our indebtedness to the last run of proactive studio Xploitation: Avco-Embassy's early-'80s out-put *(Escape from New York, Dead & Buried, The Howling, Vice Squad, Night Games, Scanners).* And once you sign on, dig our favorites: Strother Martin in *The Brotherhood of Satan* and *Sssssss;* Susan Cabot in *Sorority Girl;* Maury Dexter; Thalmus Rasulala; William Grefe's *The Hooked Generation;* and the tag-line for *Black Cobra:* "How Much Snake Can One Woman Take?"

Some of the movies in *Trash* are simon-pure masterpieces, others become preferred viewing with a whole lot of *caveat emptor.* Through Xploitation's pipeline flows veritably everything. The one commonality is an outsider tradition. From Golden Age carny shysters to Drive-In teen specialists to Porno terrorists to Straight-to-Video bums, Johnny Outsider stalks the industry and, to my taste, keeps it filthy clean. The Xploiteer is Hollywood's spook, the freak hustler in search of kicks and dollars and maybe transcendence. What are we talking about here? Some jerk-off with a yen for exposed flesh? A failed societal unit whose only hook is some fantasy he must obey? A voyeur-shaman spreading madness? A thief ripping off your time? Or just a man with a movie camera? Early on, even board-certified "respectable" directors—Friedkin, De Palma, and Scorsese—brim with the unmistakable kink of Xploitation. But they can't recapture it, because it belongs to the true outsider.

Xploitation is abnormal, but what is genuinely shocking is that its methods seem to bare the essence of human dignity, revealing it not as something that is willed or intended but just what is left after a moral or physical cataclysm has shredded everything else. An Xploitation film can be a crucible, a potently upsetting experience for those involved. After watching *Last Tango in Paris,* Brando famously quipped that he'd been raped. Similarly, Lee Holland in *Shanty Tramp,* Mel Gibson in *Mad Max,* and the entire cast of *The Texas Chainsaw Massacre* are subjected to a pattern of violation, seizures, and mental breakdown. Sometimes the violation is accompanied by great craft, evidenced in films by Peckinpah, Bava, Hitchcock, and John Carpenter. Other instances are less gentlemanly, more criminal. But an important point survives: Xploitation conquers with cruelty but need not be fiendish.

My partners and I collected these posters with the hope that we would someday run a movie theater. Now we do. You may note that some of the art seen here is worn. It's been around the block. The holes and punctures, the fissures like Big Sur, are realness crawling over fantasy, proof these movies have been shown. Appreciate this. We'd find it regrettable to present Xploitation sealed in research or linearized in chronology. We don't want to whitewash Blaxploitation or politicize "transgressive" movies. Our fetishistic contextualizing is not some academic con-job. We're more interested in nurturing mystical headspace—associative and fresh. It wouldn't be right if we soft-pedaled Xploitation's vagabondage or downplayed its blue-collar weirdness, partially because Xploitation will always be about a couple of hard-working operators getting stoned and imagining their friends doing funny, profound, possibly sick things.

If I could stress one conceptual point, it would be the "pre-irony" characteristic of these films. These days, irony eats its young; hence the surfeit of cutesy-wutesy, postmodern Clever and Soulless pictures. Xploitation offers a naïveté and dependability I find fascinating. Seek its silly charms and cheap passageways, its many jugs of innocence, and the way it pops your guts.

Ah yes, but did I mention this line from *Psyched by the 4-D Witch:* "How AWFUL and DISGUSTING and NOW WHAT!?"

— Jacques Boyreau

SEX TRASH

One great thing about Sex Trash is its candor. The friendly swell of *Campus Teasers* and payback misogyny of *The Woman Hunt* both indulge in the allure of commodified girls, raging T&A, and vulvar melodrama (narrative whose plot is driven by the question, Whom will she screw next?).

Sex Trash wants to monumentalize female presence as all "one big something or other"—the Syndicate of Bitch-Goddessness, the Ice Teat, the Voluptuosaur, the Tuff Chik, the Bubbly Daddy's Girl, the Occult Groupie. In other words, the get-go of a girl on a poster can foster fantasies from the alpha to the omega of desire. Sex Trash is frightening to contemplate for both sexes. Between the Peeping Toms and Centerfold Girls there are skulking Night Porters and armies of Teen-age Jailbait. Sex Trash is about more than the comforts of endless pulchritude. It's also a suggestion that we're all at endless risk.

Cinema-wise, this chapter covers spoiled American fatales and Euro love-zombies, yoga-stepping into a realm of sophisticated pedophilia, pottymouth savagery, and raw independence. A realm of becoming: The girl becomes cool, the slave becomes sexy, orgasm becomes entertainment, Sharon Tate becomes Dorothy Stratten, weird becomes love.

Teen-age Jailbait (date unknown) Filmakers Co.
Sorority Girl 1957 American International Pictures

The Playgirls and the Vampire 1963 Gordon/Fanfare

The Pleasure Seekers 1965 20th Century Fox

Hell's Belles 1969 American International Pictures

Caged Heat 1974 New World

The Stewardesses 1968 Stereo Vision

FOLLOWING:

Three Bad Sisters 1955 Belair/United Artists

Carmen, Baby 1967 Amsterdam Film Corp.

THREE BAD SISTERS

... out to get every thrill they could beg, buy or steal!

What
They Did
To Men
Was
Nothing
Compared
To What
They Did
To Each
Other!

CO-STARRING

MARLA ENGLISH · KATHLEEN HUGHES · SARA SHANE · JOHN BROMFIELD

| with
JESS BARKER
MADGE KENNEDY | Screenplay by
GERALD DRAYSON
ADAMS | Executive Producer
AUBREY
SCHENCK | Produced by
HOWARD W.
KOCH | Directed by
GILBERT L.
KAY | A
BEL-AIR
Production | Released
thru
UNITED
ARTISTS |

The Total Female Animal!

cool... hot...

"Carmen, Baby"

STARRING

UTA LEVKA · CLAUDE RINGER · CARL MOHNER
BARBARA VALENTINE · WALTER WILTZ · CHRISTIANE RUCKER
Screenplay by Jesse Vogel—From a story by Prospere Mérimée
an Amsterdam Film Corporation Production · Produced and Directed by RADLEY METZGER

EASTMANCOLOR and **ULTRASCOPE** · Released through AUDUBON FILMS Ⓐ

YOU READ ABOUT HER IN PLAYBOY MAGAZINE...

NOW SEE ALL OF JAYNE MANSFIELD!

UNCUT !
UNCENSORED !
EUROPEAN VERSION !

"Promises! Promises!"

starring JAYNE MANSFIELD

MARIE McDONALD

TOMMY NOONAN

A NOONAN-TAYLOR Production
Released by NTD, Inc.

Promises! Promises! 1963 NTD

Trip with the Teacher 1974 Crown International

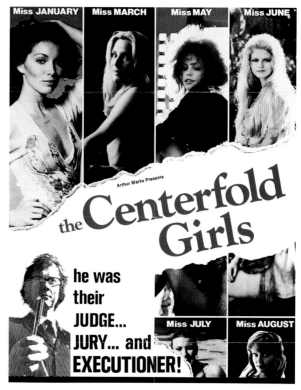

The Centerfold Girls 1974 General Film Corp.
Night Games 1980 Avco Embassy
The Stepmother 1972 Crown International

She forced her husband's son to commit the ultimate sin!!

CROWN INTERNATIONAL PICTURES presents

THE STEPMOTHER

...it's a family affair

COLOR by Deluxe R RESTRICTED Under 17 Requires Accompanying Parent or Adult Guardian

Starring
Alejandro Rey · John Anderson · Katherine Justice · Marlene Schmidt · John D. Garfield · Produced, Written & Directed by Hikmet Avedis · Executive Producer Lenke Romanzsky · Associate Producer Marlene Schmidt

Theme Song: 'Strange are The Ways Of Love' · Music by Sammy Fain · Lyrics by Paul Francis Webster · A Magic Eye of Hollywood Productions, Inc. · A Crown International Pictures Release

Hustler Squad 1976 Crown International
The Woman Hunt 1972 New World Pictures

Women are made for men... TO HUNT!

Set your sights on the Tastiest Game of all.

the WOMAN HUNT

Starring JOHN ASHLEY · PAT WOODELL · LAURIE ROSE
CHARLENE JONES · LISA TODD · SID HAIG
Produced by JOHN ASHLEY and EDDIE ROMERO · Directed by EDDIE ROMERO
A FOUR ASSOCIATES, LTD. PRODUCTION · A NEW WORLD PICTURES RELEASE
METROCOLOR

R RESTRICTED

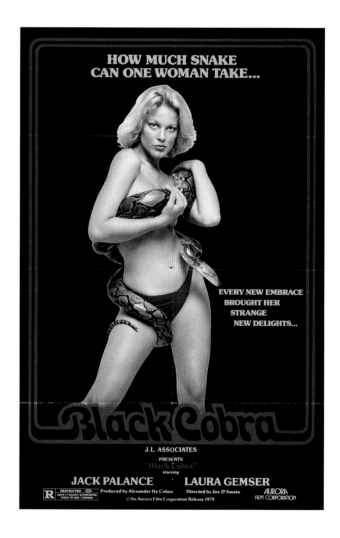

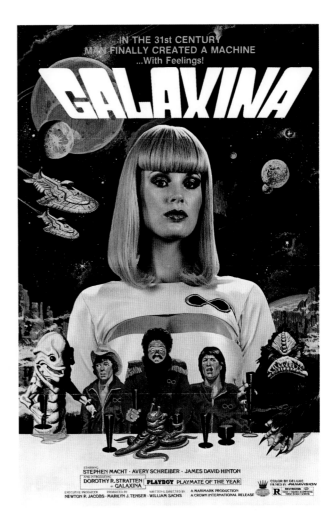

Campus Teasers (date unknown) SRC Films

Black Cobra 1979 Aurora

The Night Porter 1974 AVCO Embassy

Galaxina 1980 Crown/Marimark Prod.

...and suddenly the screams of a baby born in Hell!

WARNING! THIS MOTION PICTURE
CONTAINS THE MOST SHOCKING
SCENES THIS SIDE OF HELL!

TO THE DEVIL...
A DAUGHTER

A HAMMER/TERA ANGLO/GERMAN CO-PRODUCTION

RICHARD WIDMARK • CHRISTOPHER LEE in "TO THE DEVIL...A DAUGHTER"
Co-starring HONOR BLACKMAN • DENHOLM ELLIOTT • NASTASSJA KINSKI • ANTHONY VALENTINE • Screenplay by
CHRISTOPHER WICKING and JOHN PEACOCK • Based on the novel by DENNIS WHEATLEY • Produced by ROY SKEGGS
Directed by PETER SYKES • An EMI Film • TECHNICOLOR® • A CINE ARTISTS PICTURES RELEASE [R] RESTRICTED

To the Devil . . . A Daughter 1976 Cine Artists
Nurse Sherri 1978 Independent International

Meet SHERRI—for an evening of PLEASURE and TERROR

NURSE SHERRI

ACTION TRASH

People may argue over the influence of violent pictures upon society, but no one can doubt their colossal effect upon the imagination. A seasoned Xploiteer keeps an internal body-count, a private stash of kinetic showdowns—massive, strangely smiled-upon feats of death. There is undeniable poetry in skillfully drawn macho delirium. The speed of destruction, the price for "setting things right," it's all here in Action Trash.

Hippie-schooled odes against the Establishment (*No Blade of Grass, Damnation Alley, Escape from New York*); existentialist collision fantasies (*Vanishing Point, The Gauntlet*); numbskull exercises in conflagration (*Sweet Revenge, Killer Force*)—the roots of Action Trash feed on survival and anti-themness, the vehement dislike for organizations larger than self or family. Action Trash is obsessed with making an audience take things personally. What the genre posits is not exactly a Method-molded anti-hero, but more simply a messed-up-dude version of the perennial 'strong, silent type.' A man sold on 'desensitization' as a useful spirit-tool, an Ultimate Warrior with the android cool of Yul Brynner, or an eyepatched Kurt Russell.

Action Trash has an undiluted view of mortality. It waves off society, choosing instead to pursue its deathwish of happiness. Whether via crime, sci-fi, espionage, kung-fu, or apocalyptics, Action Trash gets the job done. Shit likes to die in this genre.

"KILL,
Kill the pusher.

KILL,
Kill the source.

KILL,
Kill the contact.

KILL"

ALEXANDER SALKIND presents STEPHEN BOYD · JEAN SEBERG · JAMES MASON · CURT JURGENS in "KILL" · Written and Directed by ROMAIN GARY
With DANIEL EMILFORK and MAURO PARENTI JOSE MARIA CAFFARELL and introducing CARLOS MONTOYA with the participation of
HENRI GARCIN · Music by BERTO PISANO and JACQUES CHAUMONT (Editions General Music—Rome) · Director of Photography EDMOND RICHARD
Executive Producer ILYA SALKIND · Produced by ALEXANDER SALKIND · EASTMANCOLOR
FROM CINERAMA RELEASING

R RESTRICTED
Under 17 requires accompanying
Parent or Adult Guardian

COPYRIGHT ©1972 CINERAMA RELEASING

72/387

Kill, Kill, Kill 1972 Cinerama
Sweet Revenge 1977 MGM/United Artists

FOLLOWING:
1997: Fuga da New York (Italy) 1981 AVCO Embassy
Escape from New York 1981 AVCO Embassy

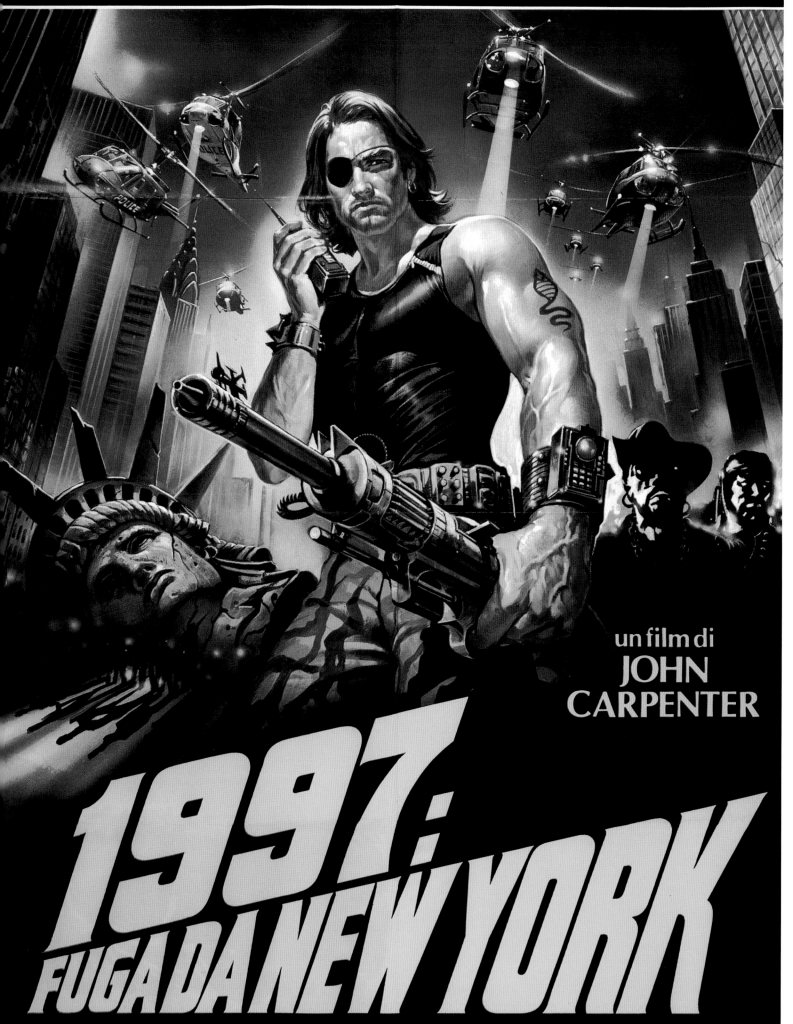

1997: NEW YORK E' UN CARCERE FORTIFICATO DI MASSIMA SICUREZZA ENTRARVI E' IMPOSSIBILE. PENSARE DI USCIRNE E' FOLLIA.

un film di
JOHN CARPENTER

1997: FUGA DA NEW YORK

JOHN CARPENTER "1997: FUGA DA NEW YORK" una produzione DEBRA HILL con KURT RUSSELL · LEE VAN CLEEF · ERNEST BORGNINE · DONALD PLEASENCE · ISAAC HAYES · SEASON HUBLEY · HARRY DEAN STANTON nel ruolo di BRAIN e ADRIENNE BARBEAU nel ruolo di MAGGIE

scritto da JOHN CARPENTER e NICK CASTLE · prodotto da LARRY FRANCO e DEBRA HILL · diretto da JOHN CARPENTER · un film CITY   Colore della TECHNOSPES

MEDUSA DISTRIBUZIONE

DOLBY STEREO

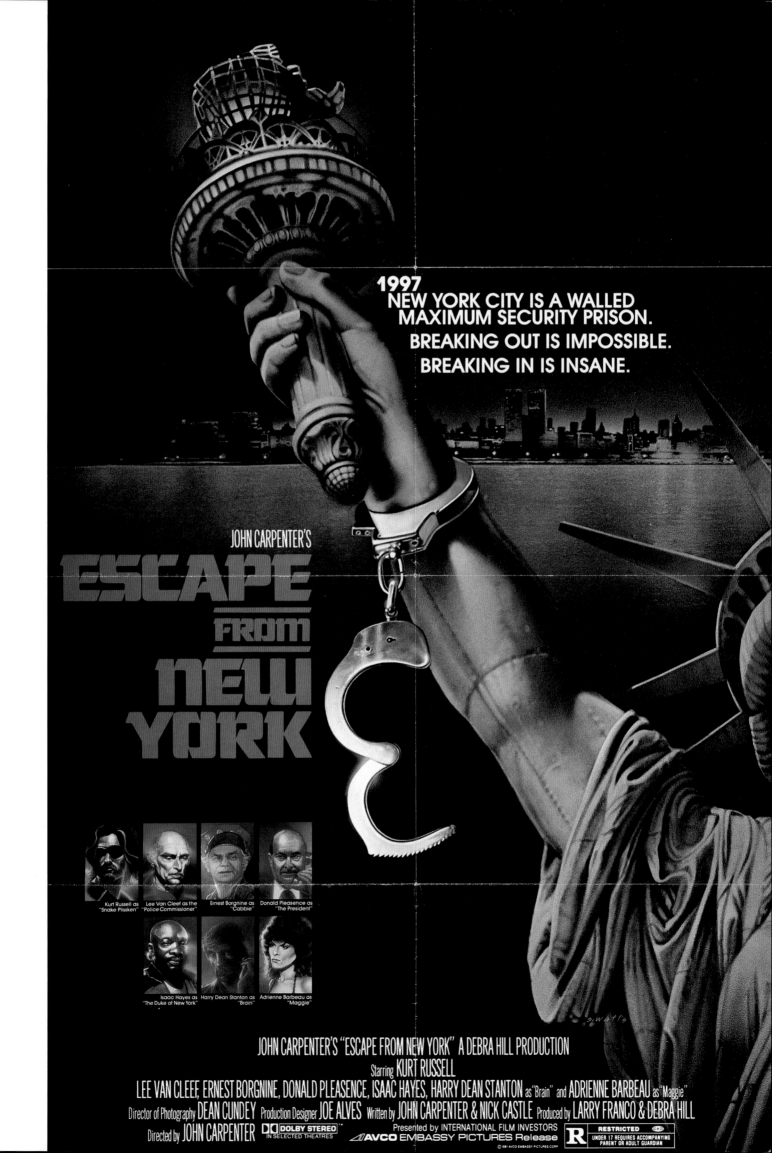

The Ultimate Warrior 1975 Warner Bros.

The Hong Kong Cat (date unknown) Hong Kong/American International Pictures

Damnation Alley 1977 20th Century Fox

YOU HAVE SEEN GREAT ADVENTURES.
YOU ARE ABOUT TO LIVE ONE.

The magnificent epic of five people who survive the nuclear holocaust
and their incredible odyssey through the nightmare world it created.

And now, you will not only see it, you will feel it,
live it—in "SOUND 360"—a revolutionary sight and sound experience.

**More than a movie.
An adventure you'll never forget**

20TH CENTURY-FOX PRESENTS
DAMNATION ALLEY

JAN-MICHAEL VINCENT   GEORGE PEPPARD   DOMINIQUE SANDA   PAUL WINFIELD

Executive Producers   Produced by
HAL LANDERS and BOBBY ROBERTS   JEROME M. ZEITMAN and PAUL MASLANSKY

Screenplay by   From the Novel by   Music by   Directed by
ALAN SHARP and LUKAS HELLER   ROGER ZELAZNY   JERRY GOLDSMITH   JACK SMIGHT

PANAVISION® COLOR BY DeLUXE®   (Patent Pending)   **PG** PARENTAL GUIDANCE SUGGESTED SOME MATERIAL MAY NOT BE SUITABLE FOR CHILDREN   © 1977 20TH CENTURY-FOX

WHEN WOMEN RULED THE EARTH!

Women Warriors as Sensuous as they are Savage.

Women Rulers as Passionate as they are Powerful.

TERENCE YOUNG'S WAR GODDESS

TERENCE YOUNG'S WAR GODDESS starring ALENA JOHNSTON & SABINE SUN guest star LUCIANA PALUZZI Music by RIZ ORTOLANI · Screenplay by RICHARD AUBREY · Story by ROBERT GRAVES & RICHARD AUBREY Scenario by DINO MAIURI, MASSIMO DE RITA & SERGE DE LA ROCHE · Produced by NINO KRISMAN Directed by TERENCE YOUNG · color by Technicolor' **R** an American International release

COPYRIGHT ©1974 AMERICAN INTERNATIONAL PICTURES, INC.

74/160

WAR GODDESS

War Goddess 1972 American International Pictures

Wonder Women 1973 General Film Corp.

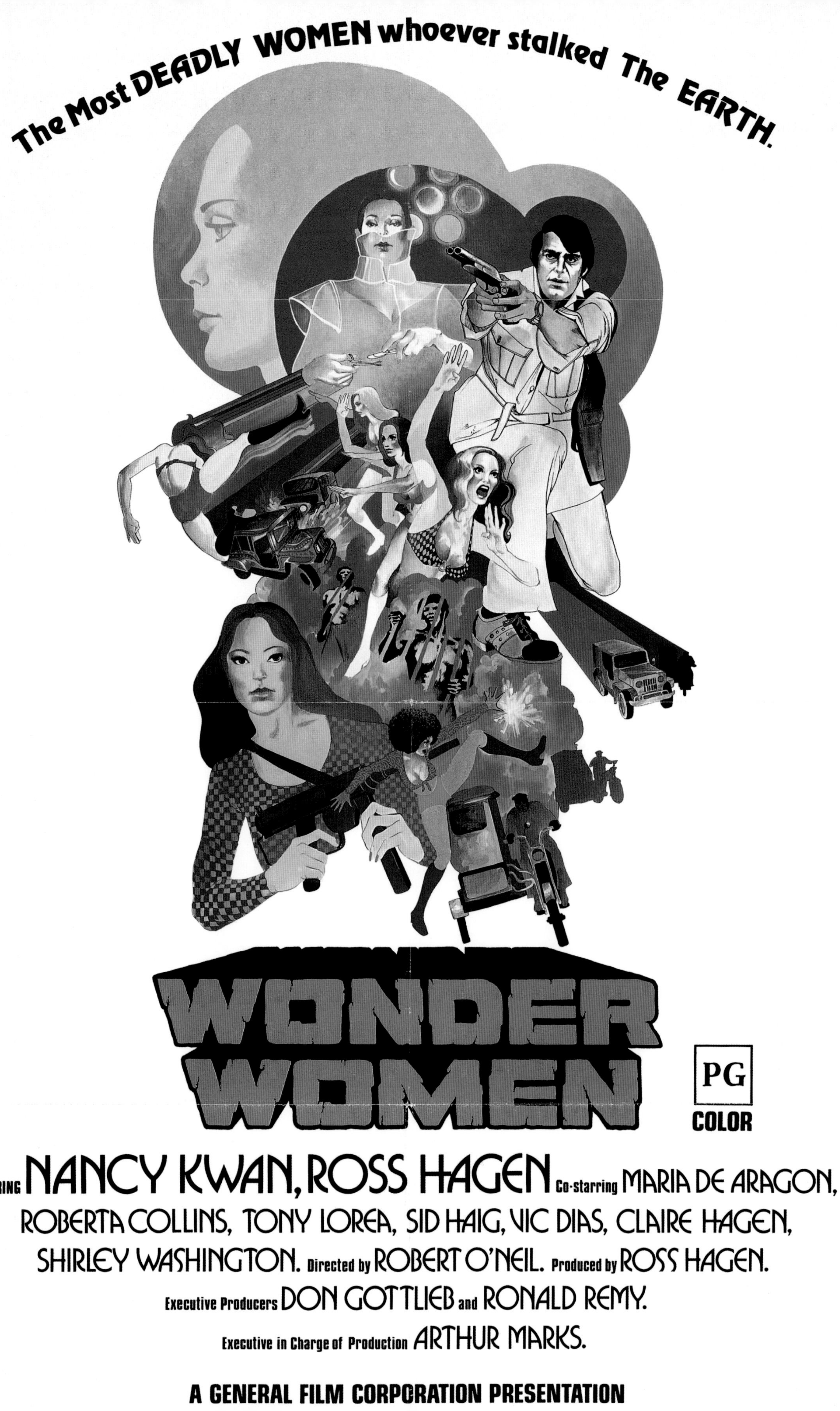
The Most DEADLY WOMEN whoever stalked The EARTH.
WONDER WOMEN
PG
COLOR
STARRING NANCY KWAN, ROSS HAGEN Co-starring MARIA DE ARAGON,
ROBERTA COLLINS, TONY LOREA, SID HAIG, VIC DIAS, CLAIRE HAGEN,
SHIRLEY WASHINGTON. Directed by ROBERT O'NEIL. Produced by ROSS HAGEN.
Executive Producers DON GOTTLIEB and RONALD REMY.
Executive in Charge of Production ARTHUR MARKS.
A GENERAL FILM CORPORATION PRESENTATION

**Yesterday, they were decent people letting their environment die.
Now, they are savages, killing to keep themselves alive.**

NO BLADE OF GRASS

Metro-Goldwyn-Mayer presents "NO BLADE OF GRASS" Starring Nigel Davenport /Jean Wallace /Anthony May /Screenplay by Sean Forestal and Jefferson Pascal /Produced and Directed by Cornel Wilde /Filmed in Panavision® and Metrocolor®

RESTRICTED Under 17 requires accompanying Parent or Adult Guardian

 MGM

The psychotic killer, the young heiress...
the kidnapping
that becomes
a love story.

THE GRISSOM GANG

ABC PICTURES CORP. PRESENTS "THE GRISSOM GANG"
AN ASSOCIATES AND ALDRICH COMPANY PRODUCTION
STARRING KIM DARBY   SCOTT WILSON   TONY MUSANTE   ROBERT LANSING CO-STARRING IRENE DAILEY AND CONNIE STEVENS AS ANNA
MUSIC BY GERALD FRIED   SCREENPLAY BY LEON GRIFFITHS   FROM A NOVEL BY JAMES HADLEY CHASE   PRODUCED AND DIRECTED BY ROBERT ALDRICH
A SUBSIDIARY OF THE AMERICAN BROADCASTING COMPANIES, INC. METROCOLOR® DISTRIBUTED BY 20th CENTURY-FOX FILM CORPORATION

No Blade of Grass 1971 MGM
The Grissom Gang 1971 ABC Pictures/Aldrich

Dirty Mary Crazy Larry/Vanishing Point 1975 20th Century Fox

Vanishing Point 1971 20th Century Fox

Dirty Mary Crazy Larry 1973 20th Century Fox

They were professionals who killed for hire.

But the man who hunted them killed for pleasure!

SAMUEL Z. ARKOFF presents

**TELLY SAVALAS · PETER FONDA
HUGH O'BRIAN · O.J. SIMPSON · MAUD ADAMS**
and **CHRISTOPHER LEE**

in **KILLER FORCE**

an **American International Release**

R	**RESTRICTED**

screenplay by MICHAEL WINDER, VAL GUEST and GERALD SANFORD · produced by NAT and PATRICK WACHSBERGER · directed by VAL GUEST
music composed by GEORGES GARVARENTZ — published by CHAPPELL-AZNAVOUR, LTD. · services by GEM SERVICE COMPANY · color prints by MOVIELAB

COPYRIGHT ©1975 AMERICAN INTERNATIONAL PICTURES, INC.

76/4

KILLER FORCE

Embassy 1972 K-Tel

Killer Force 1975 American International Pictures

Mad Max 1980 American International Pictures
The Gauntlet 1977 Warner Bros.

CLINT EASTWOOD in A MALPASO COMPANY FILM "THE GAUNTLET" Starring SONDRA LOCKE

Written by MICHAEL BUTLER and DENNIS SHRYACK • Produced by ROBERT DALEY • Directed by CLINT EASTWOOD • Music JERRY FIELDING • PANAVISION® • Color by DELUXE®

UNDER 17 REQUIRES ACCOMPANYING
PARENT OR ADULT GUARDIAN

© 1977 Warner Bros. Inc.

From Warner Bros.,
A Warner Communications Company

A Harvey Bernhard–Gabriel Katzka P
Music by Les Baxter · Executiv
Based on the Novel by Edward Levy

HORROR TRASH

From Action Trash's turf wars of Thanatos, we hit the cornucopia of Horror Trash, where death has a more burlesque gig. Instead of the warrior-stoics of Action Trash, the populace of Horror Trash is hysterical, vampy, exhibitionistic, vulgar.

The nervous energy tearing through this chapter shows you why Horror Trash denotes Catharsis. Every which way, from the veiny, organ-donor font of *Suspiria* to the cobra tonsils of *Sssssss*, from the cat scratch of *The Howling* to the tabloid silhouette of *The Beast Within*, THE motif in Horror Trash is a mouth furnished with a scream. Even the lethal vector of *Willard* (rendered in pointillistic black and white) vibrates with a rodent yowl.

Whether one is particularly excited by eyeballs, worms, frogs, victim scenarios, butchery, Dracula's dog, or Paul Williams as little lord Lucifer—the best moments in Horror Trash confidently expropriate Beauty from pretty girls and sun-garbed things. The other great moments make their mark with a good deal more desperate idiocy. This genre demands a *Ghoulies*.

Horror Trash is a force fantastic. It pours over our body politic and through the dams of our subconscious, continuously tapping who knows what except that it must scream or snort moistly.

THERE'S MORE TO THE LEGEND THAN MEETS... THE THROAT!

CROWN INTERNATIONAL PICTURES Presents

Dracula's Dog

NAT COHEN presents An ALBERT BAND, FRANK RAY PERILLI, VIC PRODUCTIONS FILM "DRACULA'S DOG"

Starring MICHAEL PATAKI • REGGIE NALDER • JOSE FERRER

Written by FRANK RAY PERILLI • Produced by ALBERT BAND & FRANK RAY PERILLI

Directed by ALBERT BAND • Color Prints by DELUXE

A CROWN INTERNATIONAL PICTURES RELEASE

R RESTRICTED
Under 17 requires accompanying Parent or Adult Guardian

WHAT IS IT?

FOR THE ANSWER SEE

WEREWOLF IN A GIRLS' DORMITORY

(THE GHOUL IN SCHOOL)

Dracula's Dog 1978 Crown International

Werewolf in a Girls' Dormitory 1963 MGM

This was the night of the
CRAWLING TERROR!

An AMERICAN INTERNATIONAL Release

THE EDGAR LANSBURY-JOSEPH BERUH Production

STARRING DON · PATRICIA R.A. · JEAN

'SQUIRM' SCARDINO · PEARCY · DOW · SULLIVAN

EXECUTIVE PRODUCERS EDGAR LANSBURY & JOSEPH BERUH

PRODUCER GEORGE MANASSE · MUSIC COMPOSED BY ROBERT PRINCE

COLOR BY MOVIELAB

WRITTEN AND DIRECTED BY JEFF LIEBERMAN

R RESTRICTED Under 17 Requires Accompanying Parent or Adult Guardian

"CORRUPTION" IS NOT A WOMAN'S PICTURE!

where will the bodies turn up next? ...under a car seat? ...in a valise?

...or in a deep-freeze?

THEREFORE: NO WOMAN WILL BE ADMITTED ALONE TO SEE THIS SUPER-SHOCK FILM!!

COLUMBIA PICTURES PRESENTS PETER CUSHING AND SUE LLOYD IN **"CORRUPTION"**

Squirm 1976 American International Pictures
Corruption 1968 Columbia

Where your
nightmares end...

WILLARD

begins.

This is the <u>one</u> movie
you should not see alone.

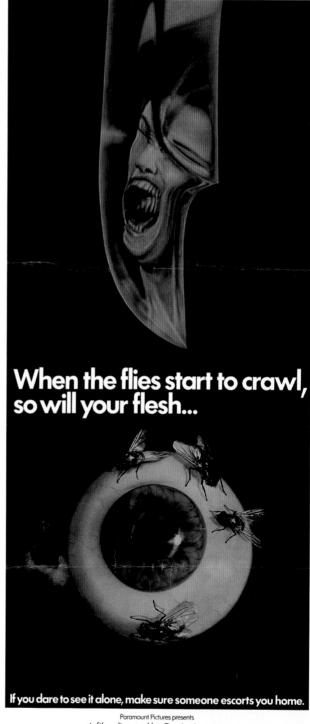

When the flies start to crawl,
so will your flesh...

If you dare to see it alone, make sure someone escorts you home.

Paramount Pictures presents

A film directed by Dario Argento

"Four Flies on Grey Velvet"

with
Michael Brandon Mimsy Farmer Jean Pierre Marielle Francine Racette
and Bud Spencer   Music scored by Ennio Morricone   Produced by Salvatore Argento
Seda Spettacoli - Rome and Universal Prod. France-Paris Technicolor® - Techniscope®
A Paramount Picture

Willard 1971 Cinerama

Four Flies on Grey Velvet 1972 Paramount

Phantom of the Paradise 1974 20th Century Fox

He's been maimed and framed, beaten, robbed and mutilated. But they still can't keep him from the woman he loves.

PHANTOM OF THE PARADISE

THE MOST HIGHLY ACCLAIMED HORROR PHANTASY OF OUR TIME

TWENTIETH
CENTURY-FOX
FILM CORPORATION

Cleaver. Cleaver. Chop. Chop. First the mom and then the pop. Then we'll get the pretty girl. We'll get her right between the curl.

National General Pictures *presents*
The Boulting Brothers' *Production*

Starring   *Also Starring*
Hayley Mills   **Hywel Bennett**   Billie Whitelaw   Phyllis Calvert

Guest Star Frank Finlay with Barry Foster   Salmaan Peer   Directed by **Roy Boulting**   Produced by **George W. George** and **Frank Granat**

Screenplay by Leo Marks and Roy Boulting **Technicolor'**   A National General Pictures Release

a New Excitement in Entertainment

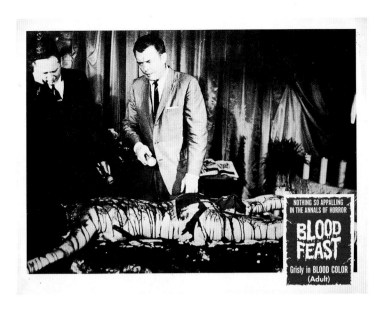

Twisted Nerve 1969 National General Pictures

Blood Feast 1963 Box Office Spectaculars

Werewolves on Wheels 1971 Fanfare

The Astro-Zombies 1968 Genie

Blue Sunshine (Belgium) 1978 Cinema Shares

The Brotherhood of Satan 1971 Columbia

The Dunwich Horror 1970 American International Pictures

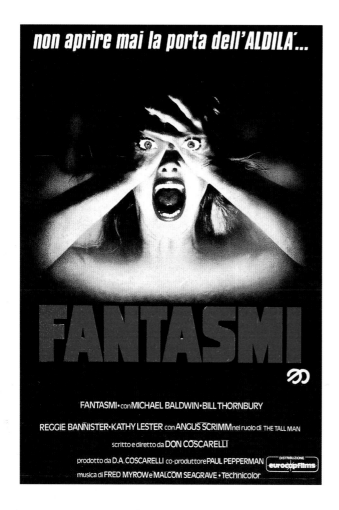

Fantasmi (Italy) 1979 AVCO Embassy
The Howling 1980 AVCO Embassy
Suspiria 1977 International Classics

The Only Thing More Terrifying
Than The Last 12 Minutes Of This Film
Are The First 92.

Once You've Seen It
You Will Never Again Feel Safe In The Dark

it's loose again eating everyone!

SON OF BLOB

BLOOD-CURDLING COLOR

BIG NEW THRILLER

GP ⬡

produced and released by
Jack H. Harris
Enterprises, Inc.

Son of Blob 1972 Jack H. Harris

Sssssss 1973 Universal

Willard 1971 Cinerama

A WILD SCIENCE FICTION NIGHTMARE.

A living, crawling hell on earth.

KINGDOM OF THE SPIDERS

A LARRY WOOLNER / MICKEY ZIDE Presentation

starring

WILLIAM SHATNER

co-starring   and introducing

TIFFANY BOLLING • WOODY STRODE • ALTOVISE DAVIS

K DRESSLER • DAVID McLEAN • NATASHA RYAN • MARCY LAFFERTY • Produced by IGO KANTOR and JEFFREY M. SNELLER • Executive Producer HENRY FOWNES
enplay by RICHARD ROBINSON and ALAN CAILLOU • Directed by JOHN BUD CARDOS • An ARACHNID Production ▣ A DIMENSION PICTURES Release

Kingdom of the Spiders 1977 Dimension
Don't Open the Window 1976 Newport
Don't Look in the Basement 1973 American
International/Hallmark

FOLLOWING:
Bloodthirsty Butchers 1969 Constitution
Pieces 1981 (company unknown)

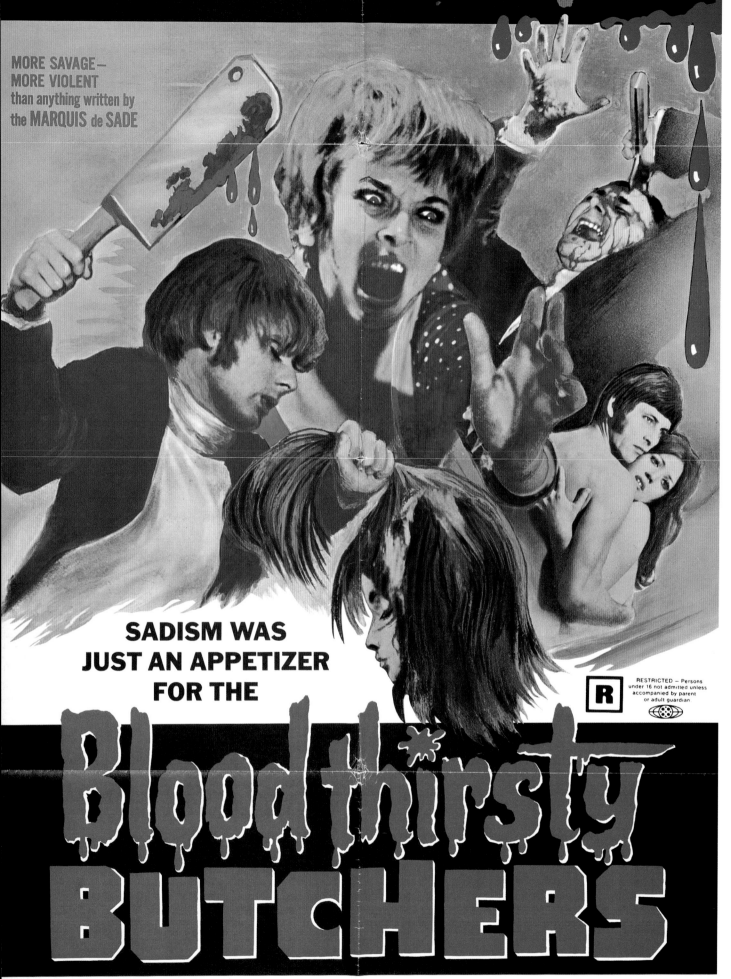

YOU DON'T HAVE TO GO TO TEXAS FOR A CHAINSAW MASSACRE!

ABSOLUTELY NO ONE UNDER 17 ADMITTED TO THIS PERFORMANCE

PIECES

IT'S EXACTLY WHAT YOU THINK IT IS!

Starring **CHRISTOPHER GEORGE PAUL SMITH**
EDMUND PURDOM LINDA DAY Music by **CAM**
Screenplay by **DICK RANDALL** & **JOHN SHADOW**
Produced by **DICK RANDALL** & **STEVE MANASIAN** Directed by **J. SIMON**

Something is alive in the Funhouse!

THE FUN HOUSE

From The Director Who Brought You The
"Texas Chain Saw Massacre"

ELIZABETH BERRIDGE COOPER HUCKABEE MILES CHAPIN SYLVIA MILES
WILLIAM FINLEY KEVIN CONWAY as the Barker in THE FUNHOUSE
Written by LARRY BLOCK Directed by TOBE HOOPER
Produced by DEREK POWER and STEVEN BERNHARDT
Executive Producers MACE NEUFELD and MARK LESTER

  **R** RESTRICTED
UNDER 17 REQUIRES ACCOMPANYING
PARENT OR ADULT GUARDIAN

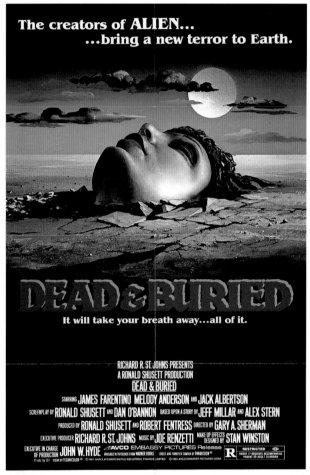

The Funhouse 1981 Universal

Ghoulies 1985 Empire Pictures

Dead & Buried 1981 AVCO Embassy

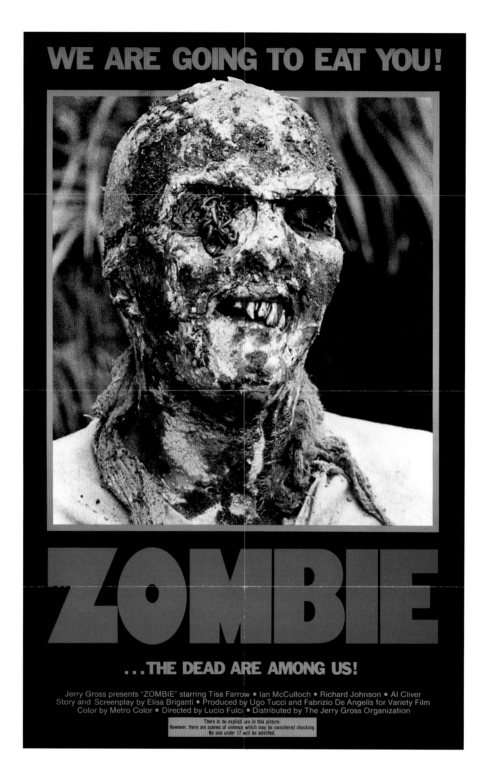

Zombie 1980 Jerry Gross Organization

The Beast Within 1982 MGM/United Artists

This motion picture contains scenes of extremely graphic and violent horror.

WARNING!

THE BEAST WITHIN

A Harvey Bernhard–Gabriel Katzka Production "The Beast Within" Ronny Cox · Bibi Besch · Paul Clemens · Don Gordon
Music by Les Baxter · Executive Producer Jack B. Bernstein · Screen Story and Screenplay by Tom Holland
Based on the Novel by Edward Levy · Produced by Harvey Bernhard and Gabriel Katzka · Directed by Philippe Mora

820025

GROOVY TRASH

Groovy is a sound: It begins growling, then funnels into an "ooh" of admiration, then ascends into a brassy, culminating slice of insight. Groovy is the onomatopoeia of '60s–'70s worldviews. That said, we can optimize "groovy" for today's consumption: 1) All drugs are groovy. Right now, all drugs, somewhere in various corners of the Xploitation canon, are in the process of seeming groovy. 2) Kris Kristofferson, clean-shaven in *Cisco Pike,* is groovy. 3) Pretentious counterculture exposés like *WUSA* are groovy, and truly pretentious counterculture exposés from England like *Privilege* are even groovier. 4) Matt Helm and Diabolik are groovy (which makes James Bond definitely ungroovy). An honorary groovy is hereby bestowed upon *The Creation of the Humanoids*, Andy Warhol's favorite film.

In fact, we'd be remiss if we didn't poke the copious underbelly of Groovy Trash, for it secretes a vital slime factor—a nasty, energizing grumble of unholier-than-thou posturing. Best exemplified by the Outlaw Biker genre, this alliance of alternative and scum chic is simply, for better or worse, groovy. Bizarrely, the Biker genre shows up in every chapter in *Trash.*

So many groovy things to call groovy, but in summation, if we were to theorize Groovy Trash, some coordinates to chart would be a post-Noir evolution of beatnik sabotage, psychedelic drug salvation, generation-gap politics, tainted love, and cult sleaze. So if you don't totally understand what I'm talking about in this chapter, then you are completely groovy.

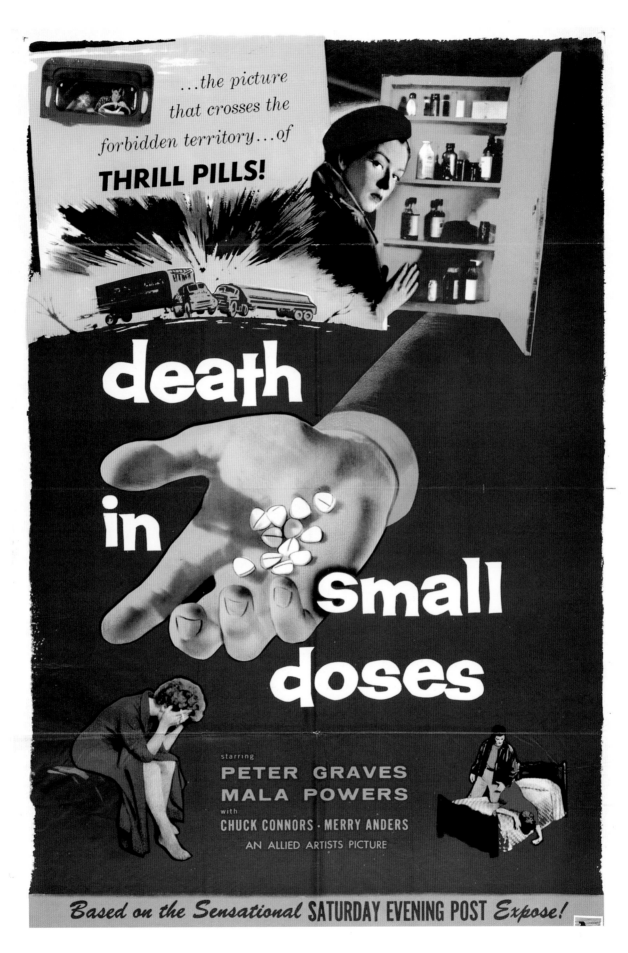

Fonda Festival 1970 American International Pictures
Death in Small Doses 1957 Allied Artists

The Sorcerers 1967 Allied Artists

More 1969 Warner Bros.

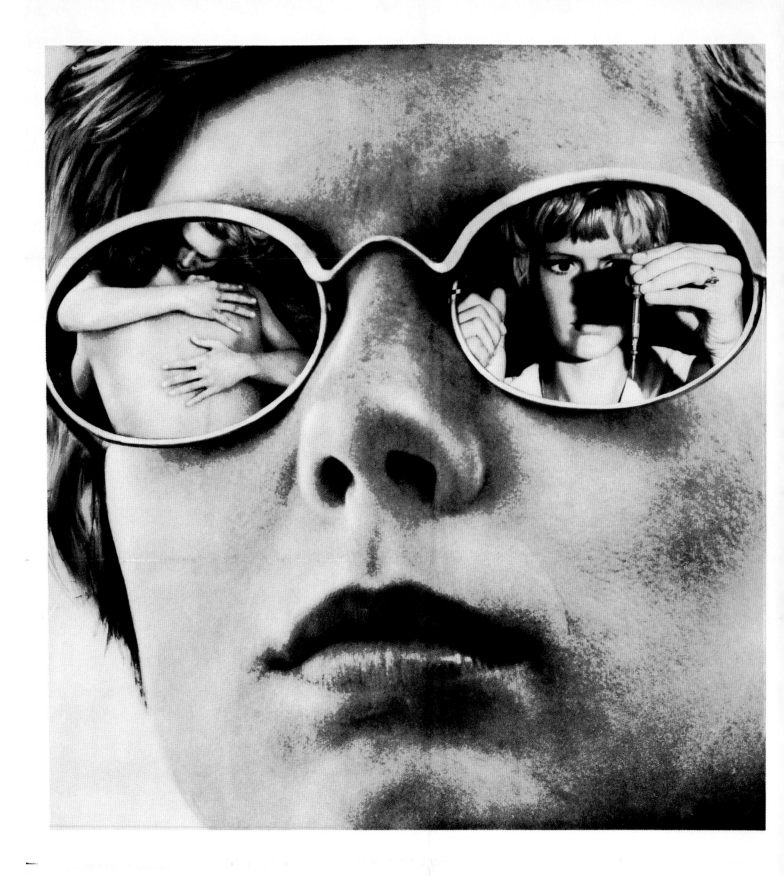

more

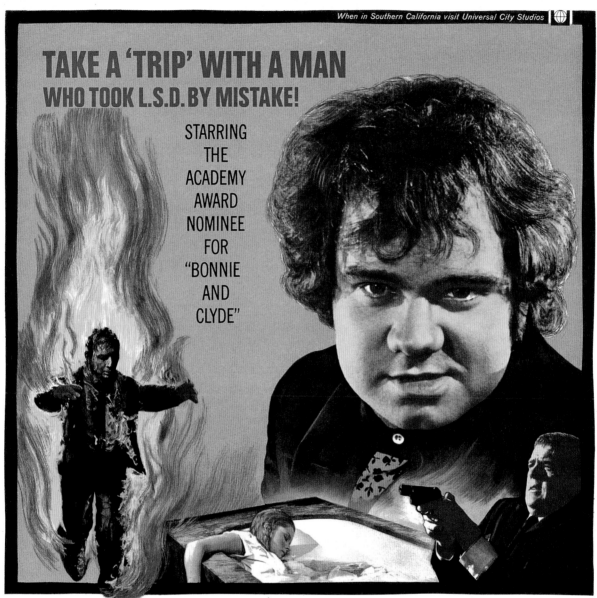

TAKE A 'TRIP' WITH A MAN
WHO TOOK L.S.D. BY MISTAKE!

STARRING
THE
ACADEMY
AWARD
NOMINEE
FOR
"BONNIE
AND
CLYDE"

A UNIVERSAL PICTURE "JIGSAW" in TECHNICOLOR®

STARRING

MICHAEL J. POLLARD·BRADFORD DILLMAN·HOPE LANGE
PAT HINGLE·SUSAN SAINT JAMES and HARRY GUARDINO

Screen story and Screenplay by QUENTIN WERTY · Based on a Screenplay by PETER STONE · Directed by JAMES GOLDSTONE · Produced by RANALD MacDOUGALL

Suggested For Mature Audiences

Jigsaw 1968 Universal

Mondo Mod 1967 Timely Motion Pictures

FOLLOWING:

The Sadist 1963 Fairway International

Pretty Poison 1968 20th Century Fox

A HUMAN VOLCANO OF UNPREDICTABLE TERROR!

NEVER BEFORE
A MOTION PICTURE
RAMPACKED WITH...

SUSPENSE...
TERROR...
SUDDEN SHOCK,
AS *THE*

Sadist

STARRING
ARCH HALL, JR.

CO-STARRING

HELEN HOVEY · RICHARD ALDEN
MARILYN MANNING · DON RUSSELL

Written and Directed by JAMES LANDIS

Produced by L. STEVEN SNYDER

A FAIRWAY-INTERNATIONAL
IMPACT PICTURE!

WHAT FIENDISH PASSION TWISTED HIS MIND—MADE HIM TORMENT, TORTURE, KILL?

20TH CENTURY-FOX Presents
A LAWRENCE TURMAN PRODUCTION

"Pretty Poison"

Did you ever see two kids like Dennis and Sue Ann? We think not...

Wait till you see what they do to his aunt—to the night watchman—to her mother.

STARRING
ANTHONY PERKINS · TUESDAY WELD
PRODUCED BY MARSHAL BACKLAR and NOEL BLACK · DIRECTED BY NOEL BLACK · SCREENPLAY BY LORENZO SEMPLE, JR. · COLOR BY DeLUXE
MUSIC BY JOHNNY MANDEL · BASED ON THE NOVEL BY STEPHEN GELLER · SUGGESTED FOR MATURE AUDIENCES

The President's Analyst 1967 Paramount

Skidoo 1968 Sigma/Paramount

Candy 1968 Cinerama

Love in the fifth dimension

20th Century-Fox Presents

JOHN BRYAN's production

THE TOUCHABLES

Starring JUDY HUXTABLE · ESTHER ANDERSON · MARILYN RICKARD · KATHY SIMMONDS
and DAVID ANTHONY Produced by JOHN BRYAN · Directed by BOB FREEMAN · Screenplay by IAN LA FRENAIS
Color by De Luxe

SUGGESTED FOR
MATURE AUDIENCES

Original soundtrack album available on 20th Century Fox Records.

The Touchables 1968 20th Century Fox

Cisco Pike 1971 Columbia

Free Grass 1970 Hollywood Star Pictures

Psych-Out 1968 American International Pictures

Simon—King of the Witches 1971 Fanfare Corporation

THE EVIL SPIRIT MUST CHOOSE EVIL...

THE BLACK MASS...THE SPELLS...THE INCANTATIONS... THE CURSES...THE CEREMONIAL SEX...

JOE SOLOMON presents

SIMON-KING of the WITCHES

METROCOLOR

Starring
ANDREW PRINE · BRENDA SCOTT and GEORGE PAULSIN · NORMAN BURTON

GERALD YORK with ULTRA VIOLET · Executive Producer JOE SOLOMON · Produced by DAVID HAMMOND
Associate Producer THOMAS J. SCHMIDT · Directed by BRUCE KESSLER · Screenplay by ROBERT PHIPPENY · Music Composed and Conducted by STU PHILLIPS

PRODUCED AND RELEASED BY
THE FANFARE CORPORATION

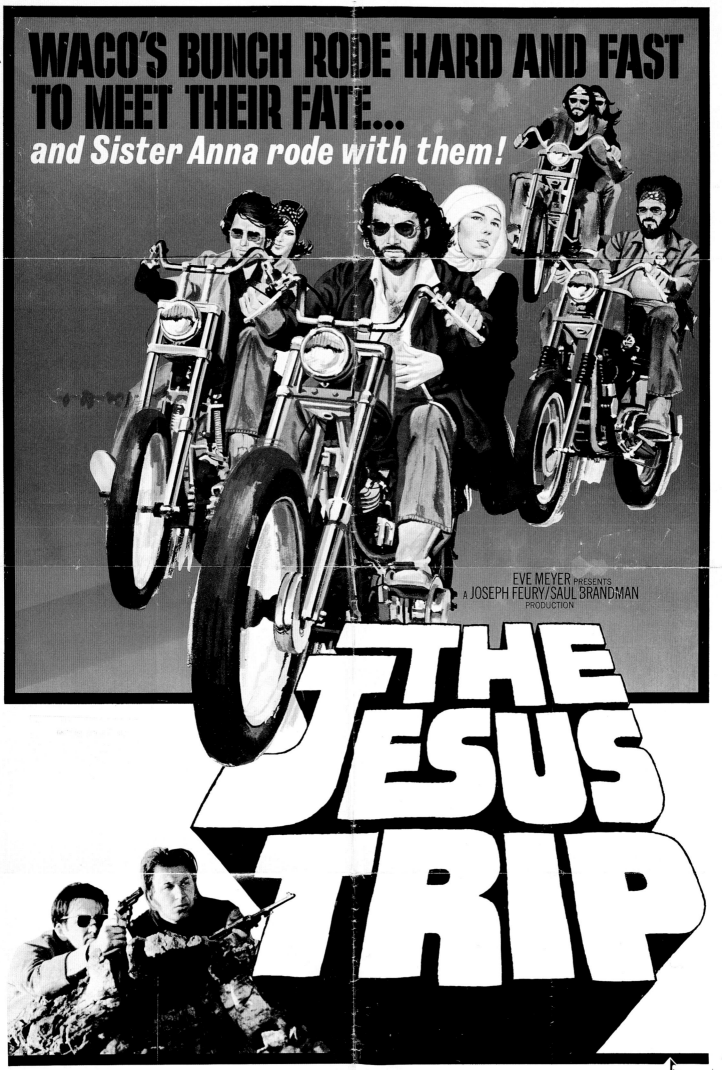

WACO'S BUNCH RODE HARD AND FAST TO MEET THEIR FATE...
and Sister Anna rode with them!

EVE MEYER PRESENTS
A JOSEPH FEURY/SAUL BRANDMAN PRODUCTION

THE JESUS TRIP

Starring TIPPY WALKER · ROBERT PORTER · BILLY "GREEN" BUSH Co-starring DIANA IVERSON · VIRGIL FRYE · CARMEN ARGENZIANO · WALLY STRAUSS as Jasper
Executive Producer SAUL BRANDMAN · Produced by JOSEPH FEURY · Written by RICHARD POSTON
Directed by RUSS MAYBERRY · COLOR

GP ALL AGES ADMITTED
Parental Guidance Suggested

Released by EMCO FILMS INC

The Jesus Trip 1971 Emco
The Pusher 1959 United Artists
The Pusher 1959 United Artists

When in Southern California visit Universal City Studios

THE RAW,
SHOCKING MOVIE
OF A
POP SINGER
WHO MAKES IT BIG!

UNIVERSAL PRESENTS the JOHN HEYMAN / PETER WATKINS PRODUCTION

PRIVILEGE

TECHNICOLOR®

Co-starring
PAUL JONES · JEAN SHRIMPTON
with
WILLIAM JOB · MARK LONDON · JEREMY CHILD · MAX BACON

Screenplay by NORMAN BOGNER · From an original story by JOHNNY SPEIGHT · Directed by PETER WATKINS · Associate Producer TIMOTHY BURRILL
Produced by JOHN HEYMAN · A WORLDFILM SERVICES LTD. / MEMORIAL ENTERPRISES LTD. PRODUCTION · A UNIVERSAL RELEASE

Privilege 1967 Universal
WUSA 1970 Paramount

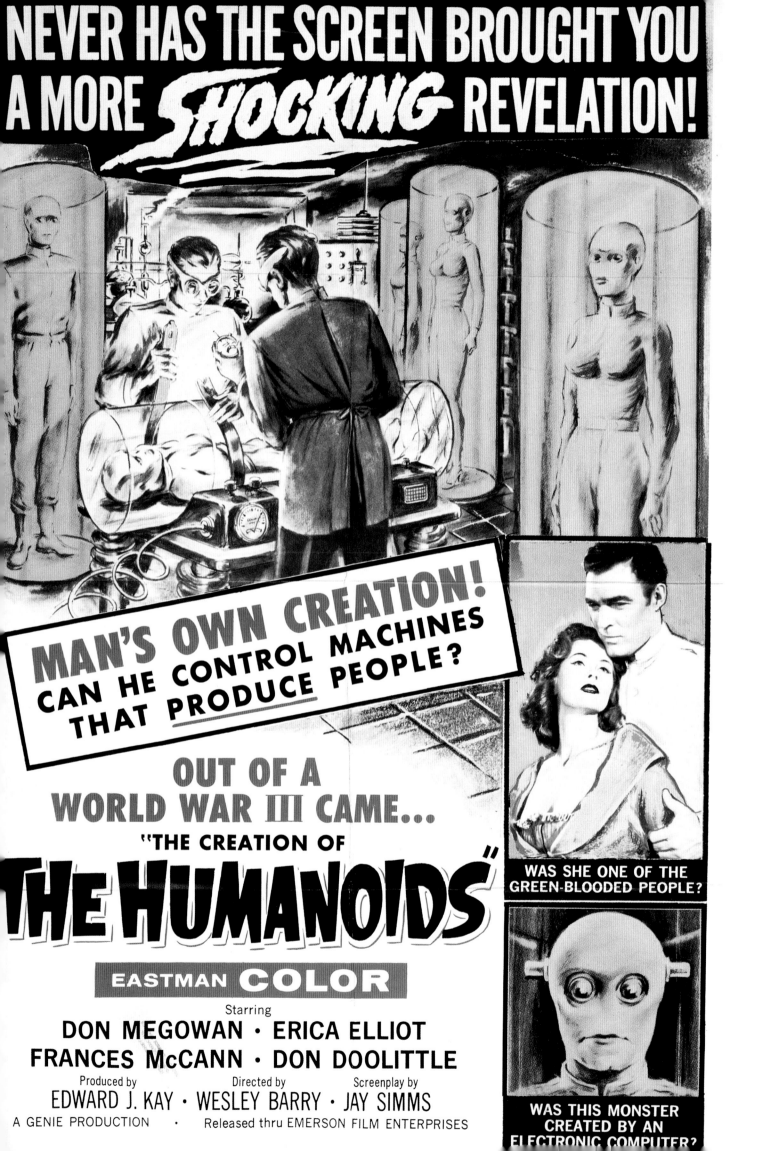

The Creation of the Humanoids 1962 Genie/Emerson Film

The People Next Door 1970 AVCO Embassy

The Pink Angels 1971 Crown International

The Wrecking Crew 1968 Columbia
Danger: Diabolik! 1968 Paramount

UNE PRODUCTION DINO DE LAURENTIIS

DANGER: DIABOLIK!

GEVAAR: DIABOLIK!

avec
JOHN PHILLIP LAW . MARISA MELL . MICHEL PICCOLI . ADOLFO CELI
CLAUDIO GORA . CATERINA BORATTO . GIULIO DONNINI . ANNIE GORASSINI
RENZO PALMER . MARIO DONEN . ANDREA BOSIC . LUCIA MODUGNO
et avec **TERRY THOMAS**
Mise en scène de **MARIO BAVA**
Une co-production franco-italienne MARIANNE PRODUCTIONS (PARIS) DINO DE LAURENTIIS CINEMATOGRAFICA (ROME) **EN COULEURS**

IMPR. LICHTERT - Bruxelles 7

RACE TRASH

Seventies Blaxploitation's mythic types—with their comic book heroism, saturated folly, healthy fury, and the all-important costume of urban realism—partook in an outbreak of outrage that, in turn, revealed sibling Whitesploitation. In haiku paraphrase, Blaxploitation is a fantasy of gaining control. Whitesploitation is a fantasy of losing control.

In Borgesian terms, "every man is two men," and conversely two men may become one. The universal joint in their mutual power train is evoked in this chapter through a paradoxical powwow of racial doubles—I mean, just look at *The Thing with Two Heads.*

Let's preview some of the more surreal links: *The Master Gunfighter*'s explicit promotion of a Billy Jack/Superfly rivalry toys with the magnitude of Godzilla vs. King Kong; the coupling of *The Omega Man* and *Black Like Me* suggests a bond between being a "last man" and a "racial impostor"; the redneck gumption of Jan-Michael Vincent and Burt "Gator" Reynolds holds a bag similar to the head of

They transplanted a WHITE BIGOT'S HEAD onto a SOUL BROTHER'S BODY!

The doctor blew it—the most fantastic medical experiment of the age. And now, with the fights, the Fuzz, the chicks and the choppers ...Man, they're really in deeeeep trouble!

SAMUEL Z. ARKOFF Presents

Ray Milland and "Rosey" Grier as...

THE THING WITH TWO HEADS

A Saber Production   An American International Release

CO-STARRING
DON MARSHALL · ROGER PERRY · KATHY BAUMANN and CHELSEA BROWN as "Lila"

COLOR by DE LUXE

PG PARENTAL GUIDANCE
May not be suitable for pre-teenagers

PRODUCED BY
WES BISHOP · JOHN LAWRENCE · LEE FROST · LEE FROST & WES BISHOP and JAMES GORDON WHITE · LEE FROST & WES BISHOP
EXECUTIVE PRODUCER   DIRECTED BY   SCREENPLAY BY   STORY BY

© 1972 American International Pictures, Inc.

72/274

The Thing with Two Heads 1972 Saber/American International Pictures
The Master Gunfighter 1975 Avondale, Billy Jack Enterprises

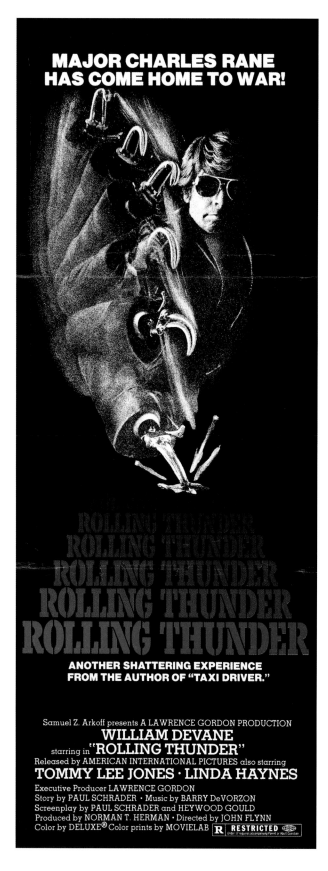

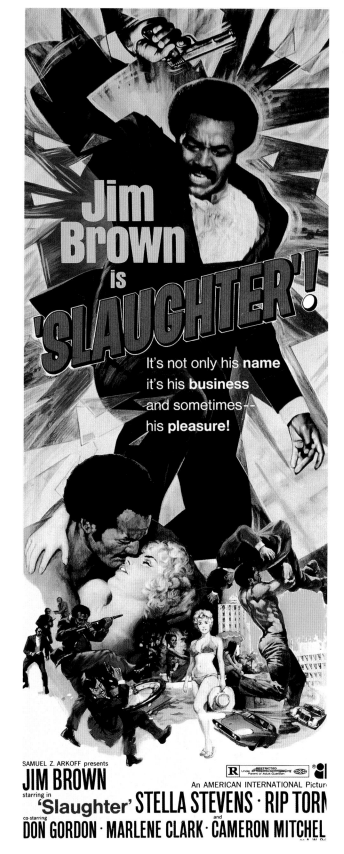

Rolling Thunder 1977 American International Pictures

Slaughter 1972 American International Pictures

Black Girl 1972 Cinerama

Straw Dogs 1971 ABC/Cinerama

She's
got
to cut
it...
or cut out.

She's a

Black Girl

...your girl.

Screenplay by J. E. Franklin based on her play
Directed by Ossie Davis

Cinerama Releasing presents a Lee Savin production **"Black Girl"**
Starring Brock Peters Louise Stubbs Claudia McNeil
Leslie Uggams as Netta Special guest Ruby Dee
Also starring Peggy Pettitt Gloria Edwards Loretta Greene
Executive Producer Robert Greenberg Produced by Lee Savin
Title song sung by Betty Everett
Original sound track on Fantasy Records

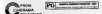

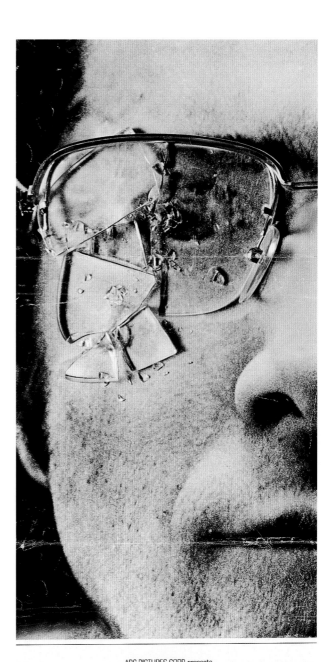

ABC PICTURES CORP. presents

DUSTIN HOFFMAN

in SAM PECKINPAH'S

"STRAW DOGS"

A DANIEL MELNICK Production
Starring SUSAN GEORGE as Amy
Music by JERRY FIELDING Screenplay by DAVID ZELAG GOODMAN

**THE Brother Man
in the Motherland.
Shaft is stickin' it
....all the way.**

starring
RICHARD ROUNDTREE
as
JOHN SHAFT

MGM Presents
A STIRLING SILLIPHANT–ROGER LEWIS Production
"SHAFT IN AFRICA"
Starring RICHARD ROUNDTREE · VONETTA McGEE
Written by STIRLING SILLIPHANT · Produced by ROGER LEWIS
Directed by JOHN GUILLERMIN
Metrocolor · Panavision®

Shaft in Africa 1973 MGM
Deliverance 1972 Warner Bros.

FOLLOWING:

Six Pack Annie 1975 American International Pictures
Cleopatra Jones and the Casino of Gold 1975 Run Run Shaw/Warner Bros.

This is the weekend they didn't play golf.

Deliverance

A JOHN BOORMAN FILM Starring **JON VOIGHT · BURT REYNOLDS** in "DELIVERANCE"
Co-Starring NED BEATTY · RONNY COX · Screenplay by James Dickey Based on his novel · Produced and Directed by John Boorman
PANAVISION® · TECHNICOLOR® · From Warner Bros., A Warner Communications Company **R** RESTRICTED Under 17 requires accompanying Parent or Adult Guardian

75/ 183

CLEOPATRA JONES AND THE CASINO OF GOLD

6 ft. 2 in. of dynamite explodes into action.

TAMARA DOBSON · STELLA STEVENS · CLEOPATRA JONES AND THE CASINO OF GOLD IN A RUN RUN SHAW / WILLIAM TENNANT PRODUCTION

Written and Produced by WILLIAM TENNANT   Based on characters created by MAX JULIEN   Directed by CHUCK BAIL   PANAVISION® TECHNICOLOR®   **R** RESTRICTED Under 17 requires accompanying Parent or Adult Guardian

from Warner Bros 🆆 A Warner Communications Company

Scum of the Earth 1974 Dimension

The Legend of Nigger Charley 1972 Paramount

The Klansman 1974 Paramount

WELCOME TO SCENIC ATOKA COUNTY

Pop. 10,000.
Cross burnings. Rape. Murder. Arson.
It's a great place to live
...if **THEY** let you.

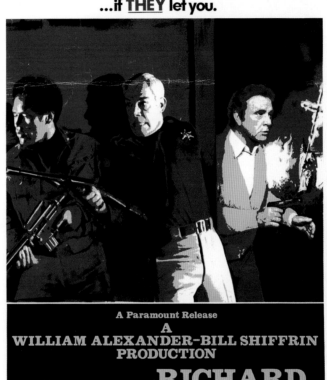

A Paramount Release

A
WILLIAM ALEXANDER–BILL SHIFFRIN
PRODUCTION

RICHARD BURTON
LEE MARVIN

A TERENCE YOUNG FILM

"THE KLANSMAN"

Co-Starring CAMERON MITCHELL
LOLA FALANA   LUCIANA PALUZZI
DAVID HUDDLESTON   LINDA EVANS
and O.J. SIMPSON as GARTH
Executive Producer BILL SHIFFRIN
Based on the Novel by WILLIAM BRADFORD HUIE
Screenplay by
MILLARD KAUFMAN and SAMUEL FULLER
Produced by WILLIAM ALEXANDER
Directed by TERENCE YOUNG
Technicolor®
A Paramount Release

R RESTRICTED
Under 17 requires accompanying
Parent or Adult Guardian

"J.C." preached love... lived violence !!

IN COLOR

J.C. AND HIS DISCIPLES WERE A GANG OF BROADS, BIKES AND BLACKS.

"J.C." starring Bill McGaha Joanna Moore Burr DeBenning Slim Pickens

Original Story and Screenplay written by Joe Thirty and William F. McGaha Music Composed by Paul Jarvis Produced and Directed by William F. McGaha An Avco Embassy Release

R RESTRICTED Under 17 requires accompanying Parent or Adult Guardian

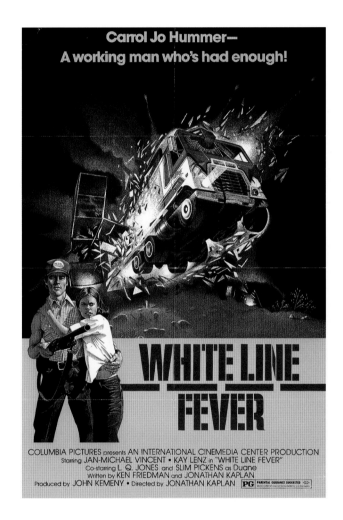

J.C. 1971 AVCO Embassy

White Line Fever 1975 Columbia

Slaughter's Big Ripoff 1973 American International Pictures

Black Like Me 1964 Continental

The Omega Man 1971 Warner Bros.

Scream Blacula Scream
1973 American International Pictures

The Soul Hustler 1973 Burton Films

Dusty and Sweets McGee 1971 Warner Bros.

Skullduggery 1970 Universal

El Salvaje Negro (Mexico) 1973 Apolo S.A.

Conquest of the Planet of the Apes 1972 20th Century Fox

GOD HELP BOBBY AND HELEN

They're in love in Needle Park

20th Century-Fox presents

the panic in needle park

starring AL PACINO and KITTY WINN

produced by DOMINICK DUNNE directed by JERRY SCHATZBERG

screenplay by JOAN DIDION and JOHN GREGORY DUNNE

a DUNNE-DIDION-DUNNE production COLOR BY DE LUXE®

The Panic in Needle Park 1971 20th Century Fox

This Rebel Breed 1960 Warner Bros.

Coffy 1973 American International Pictures

FOLLOWING:

Honky 1971 Jack H. Harris

Scorchy 1976 American International Pictures

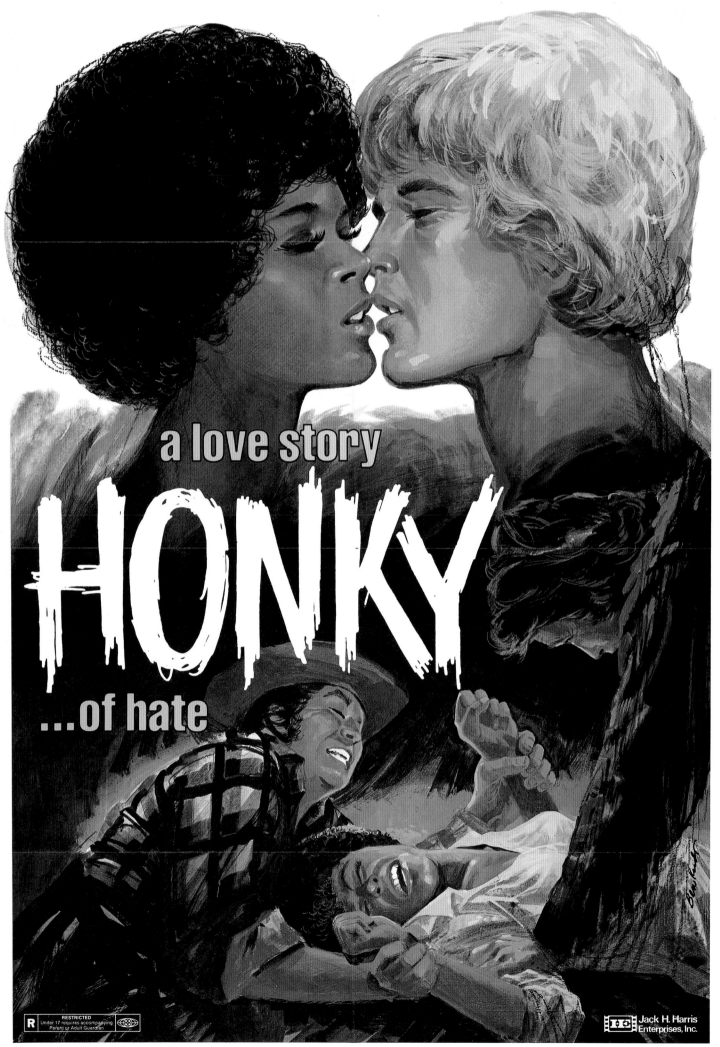

a love story

HONKY

...of hate

Jack H. Harris
Enterprises, Inc.

JACK H. HARRIS PRESENTS A GETTY-FROMKESS / STONEHENGE PRODUCTION
INTRODUCING BRENDA SYKES AND JOHN NEILSON • WRITTEN BY WILL CHANEY, BASED
ON THE NOVEL SHELIA BY GUNARD SOLBERG • EXECUTIVE PRODUCER J. RONALD GETTY
PRODUCED BY WILL CHANEY AND RON ROTH • DIRECTED BY WILLIAM A. GRAHAM

Color by De Luxe / Panavision
Music by Quincy Jones

SHE'S KILLED A MAN, BEEN SHOT AT, AND MADE LOVE TWICE ALREADY THIS EVENING... AND THE EVENING ISN'T OVER YET!

CONNIE STEVENS IS

Scorchy

(Also known as Federal Undercover Agent Jackie Parker)

also starring

CESARE DANOVA · WILLIAM SMITH

Executive Producer MARLENE SCHMIDT · Written, Produced and Directed by HIKMET AVEDIS

HICKMAR PRODUCTIONS, INC. · Color prints by Movielab

AN AMERICAN INTERNATIONAL RELEASE

R RESTRICTED
Under 17 requires accompanying Parent or Adult Guardian

Trick Baby 1973 Universal

Mr. Ricco 1975 United Artists

Bullitt 1969 Solar/Warner Bros., Seven Arts

FOLLOWING:

White Lightning 1973 United Artists

Boss Nigger 1975 Dimension

BULLITT comes to this theatre soon. That ought to shake up the place pretty good.

Not many freaky cops like BULLITT around. You look at the Italian shoes and the turtleneck and you have to wonder. You listen to the official beefs about 'personal misconduct,' 'disruptive influence,' you figure he's got to be up for trade.

But when some rare Chicago blood starts spilling in San Francisco, they give BULLITT the mop. They weren't exactly doing him a favor. But they've done a great big one for you.

STEVE McQUEEN AS 'BULLITT'

ROBERT VAUGHN

JACQUELINE BISSET · DON GORDON · ROBERT DUVALL · SIMON OAKLAND · NORMAN FELL

M SUGGESTED FOR MATURE AUDIENCES

Music by Lalo Schifrin · Screenplay by ALAN R. TRUSTMAN and HARRY KLEINER · Based on the novel "Mute Witness" by Robert L. Pike · Executive Producer ROBERT E. RELYEA · Produced by PHILIP D'ANTONI · Directed by PETER YATES. **TECHNICOLOR® FROM WARNER BROS.-SEVEN ARTS W**

Copyright © 1968 Warner Bros.—Seven Arts, Inc.

68/11

WHITE MAN'S TOWN... BLACK MAN'S LAW!

PART DEVIL...PART LEGEND...ALL MAN!

FRED WILLIAMSON as

BOSS NIGGER

with **D'URVILLE MARTIN** CO-STARRING R. G. ARMSTRONG and WILLIAM SMITH

Produced by JACK ARNOLD and FRED WILLIAMSON Directed by JACK ARNOLD

Written by FRED WILLIAMSON COLOR BY DE LUXE® Todd-AO 35

Original Motion Picture Soundtrack on "WE PRODUCE" Records and Tapes.

 A DIMENSION PICTURES RELEASE

PG PARENTAL GUI GESTED
Some rial may le for pre-teenagers

75/11

Sick or
bizarre?

eautiful

WILLIAM SHATNER'S
MYSTERIES

DOCU TRASH

The material in Docu Trash suggests that Xploitation may have a ménage à trois going with art and reality that places them both in its thrall. Docu Trash traffics in art and embezzles reality. When convenient, Docu Trash plays dumb, swearing that its trespasses are just fictional fun. But if opportunity knocks, it will inform us it has carried the very truths of existence back from the recesses of dungeons, jungles, and alien cerebra. It dares us to accept a worldview. It entertains by making us suddenly blurt, "What is this?"

Look not for themes of subject matter, but instead think of the vulnerabilities of art and reality that Docu Trash mines. We got yer' virtual-atrocity exhibits like *Survive* and *After Mein Kampf*. Plus we got yer' "separating the man from the myth" hogwash: Watch Alec Guinness nuance Hitler; get to know Che as interpreted by Omar Sharif; nod as Stuart Whitman hams up Jim Jones.

We also got yer' Mondo-exposés, those globetrotting jambalayas of eccentricity and savage desire. The Mondo rubric extends to unearthly realms, applying its fractured investigative style to *Witchcraft '70* and finally taking on the cosmos of the We-Are-Not-Alone Alien Unknown (*Chariots of the Gods, The Late Great Planet Earth*). To think that such complicated mixed messages as "entity guidance" and Biblically-wired Apocalypse derived out of the innocence of early-Mondo nudist-colony studies like *World Without Shame*—pretty wild.

"Fictional" works like *Tidal Wave* play the Docu Trash game by selling disaster-reality, an anxiety that has been refurbished by the fluidity and glibness of digital FX. And here, too, squats the Biker genre in the form of *The Losers*—which was inspired by a very real telegram from the Oakland Hell's Angels to Lyndon Johnson, volunteering to resolve the conflict in Vietnam.

The most shocking episode in the history of human survival.

SURVIVE!

CAUTION

The re-creation of the 1972 Andes plane crash and
THE SURVIVAL SCENES
may be too intense for young teenagers!

Paramount Pictures presents a Robert Stigwood and Allan Carr presentation "SURVIVE" Based on the book by Clay Blair, Jr.

Produced by Conacine and Rene Cardona, Jr. Directed by Rene Cardona, Sr. In Color A Paramount Release

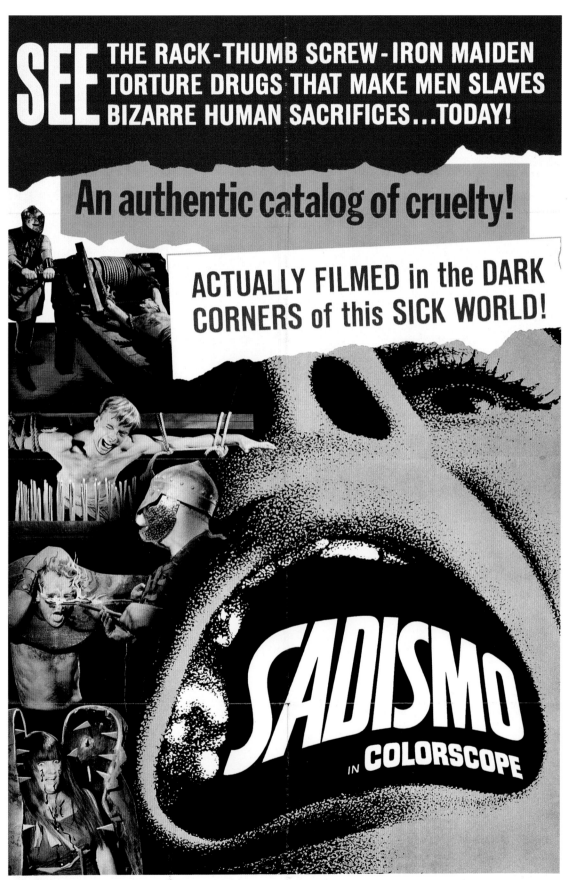

Survive! 1976 Paramount

Sadismo 1967 Trans American/American International Pictures

Hitler: The Last Ten Days 1973 Paramount

After Mein Kampf 1961 Joseph Brenner Associates, Inc.

THE REAL ▮▮▮▮▮ FILM OF HITLER'S HELL!

SEE...
Unbelieveable but true... the shocking story of Nazi atrocities!

SEE.. GREATEST SHOCK SCENE EVER FILMED!
GIRLS USED FOR "SCIENTIFIC" EXPERIMENTS WITH NEAR DEAD PRISONERS OF WAR!

SEE... HITLER'S SADISTS LEAVE THEIR SHAMELESS MARK!

NEVER BEFORE SHOWN!

HITLER IN DISGUISE IS HE STILL ALIVE?

SEE... The crematorium ovens of Majdanek, Dachau and Auschwitz

SEE... *THE RAVAGES OF HITLER ...THE RAPE OF THE WORLD!*

AFTER MEIN KAMPF

THE
LATE GREAT
PLANET EARTH

heaven and earth
will pass away, but
my words shall not pass away.
matt. 24:35

PG PARENTAL GUIDANCE SUGGESTED
SOME MATERIAL MAY NOT BE SUITABLE FOR CHILDREN

Featuring ORSON WELLES Based on the book by HAL LINDSEY with C.C. CARLSON
ROBERT AMRAM FILMS and RCR PRODUCTION Producers ROBERT AMRAM and ALAN BELKIN
Written and Directed by ROBERT AMRAM Executive Producer MICHAEL F. LEONE Asssociate Producer JOY SHELTON DAVIS
BIBLICAL SEQUENCES Written and Directed by ROLF FORSBERG Music by DANA KAPROFF
A PACIFIC INTERNATIONAL ENTERPRISES RELEASE · Color by C.F.I.

A universal force in family entertainment
production and distribution.

The Late Great Planet Earth 1976 Pacific International

Witchcraft '70 1970 Trans American

De Sade 1969 American International Pictures

Nights of Rasputin 1962 Brigadier

Viva Knievel! 1977 Warner Bros.

A SHERRILL C. CORWIN Production "VIVA KNIEVEL!"
Starring EVEL KNIEVEL · GENE KELLY
LAUREN HUTTON · RED BUTTONS
Co-Starring LESLIE NIELSEN and ERIC OLSON · CAMERON MITCHELL · ALBERT SALMI And MARJOE GORTNER as Jessie
Produced by STAN HOUGH · Directed by GORDON DOUGLAS · Executive Producer SHERRILL C. CORWIN · Story by ANTONIO SANTILLAN
Screenplay by ANTONIO SANTILLAN and NORMAN KATKOV · Technicolor ® Panavision ® Distributed by Warner Bros. A Warner Communications Company PG PARENTAL GUIDANCE SUGGESTED

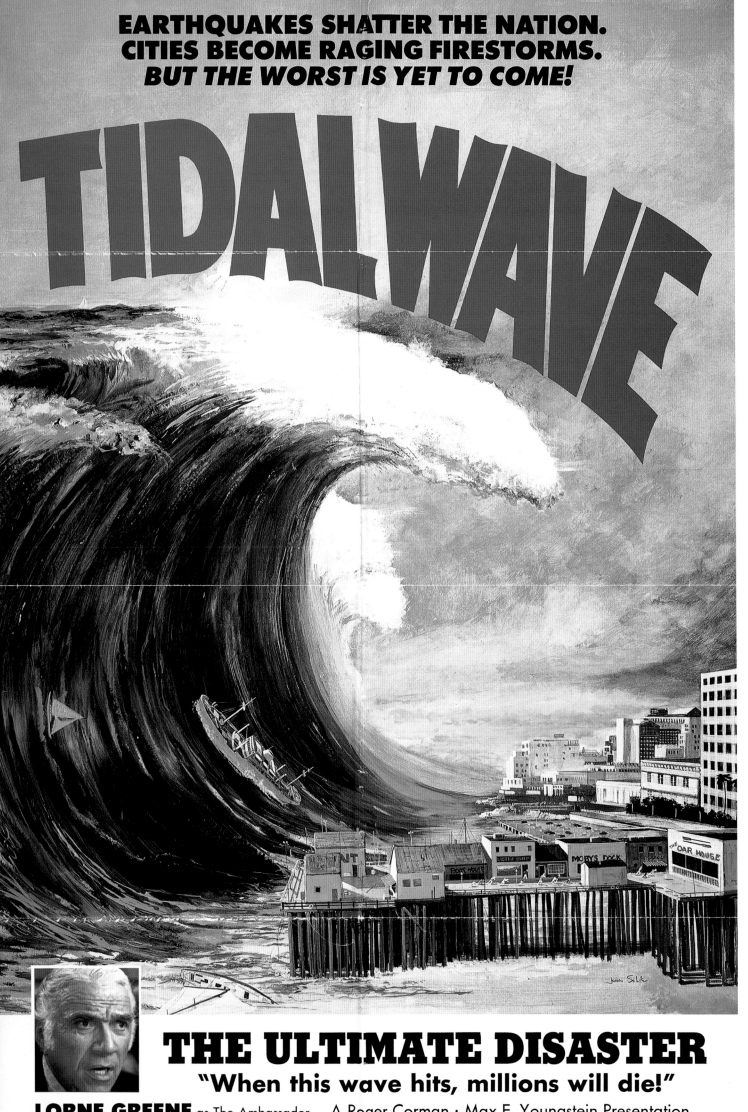

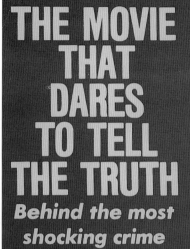

THE MOVIE THAT DARES TO TELL THE TRUTH

Behind the most shocking crime of the century!

GUYANA
CULT OF THE DAMNED

"GUYANA–CULT OF THE DAMNED" Starring STUART WHITMAN · GENE BARRY · JOHN IRELAND · JENNIFER ASHLEY and BRADFORD DILLMAN as Dr. Gary Stra
Special Appearance by JOSEPH COTTEN   Written by RENE CARDONA, JR. and CARLOS VALDEMAR · Music by JIMMIE HASKELL and ALFREDO DIAZ ORDAZ
Produced and Directed by RENE CARDONA, JR. · A UNIVERSAL RELEASE
©1979 UNIVERSAL CITY STUDIOS, INC. ALL RIGHTS RESERVED

Tidal Wave 1975 New World
Guyana: Cult of the Damned 1979 Universal

Che! 1969 20th Century Fox

Slave Trade in the World Today 1964 Continental

The Losers 1970 Fanfare Corporation

FOLLOWING:

Mysteries from Beyond Earth 1975 Pacific International

Macabro 1966 Trans American

What is the message from beyond the stars,
which has been kept secret from our world until now?
MYSTERIES FROM BEYOND EARTH
G
GENERAL AUDIENCES
All Ages Admitted
Starring Lawrence Dobkin Produced and Directed by George Gale Music by Jaime Mendoza-Nava
Screenplay by Ralph Blum, Judy Blum and Don Scioli
R.V. Coalson, Executive Producer Allan C. Pedersen, Associate Producer Color by Deluxe

SEE THE WORLD IN THE RAW!

DEATH-DEFYING ACROBATS, TRAINED BY CRUELTY AND TORTURE...TATTOOED VIRGINS
THE FORBIDDEN CITY'S STRANGE "CURES" WROUGHT IN THE NAME OF MEDICINE
SCHOOL FOR BEGGARS, WHERE CHILDREN ARE TRANSFORMED INTO MONSTERS
STRANGE JUNGLE MANHOOD RITES...MALE GEISHA GIRLS AND THEIR CUSTOMS

Sick or bizarre?

Gruesome or natural?

Beautiful or shameful?

Exotic or hideous?

Bestial or interesting?

Touching or disgusting?

JUDGE FOR YOURSELF! SEE...

"MACABRO"

...SECRETS OF THE FORBIDDEN WORLD REVEALED BY THE HIDDEN CAMERA

NARRATED BY
MARVIN MILLER ·
PRINCIPAL DIRECTION BY
ROMOLO MARCELLINI ·
RELEASED BY
TRANS AMERICAN FILMS · IN **TECHNICOLOR**®

WAS GOD AN ASTRONAUT?
The Amazing Story Of Earth's Unsolved Mysteries.

Chariots of the Gods 1969 Blake Films/Sunn Classics

Mysteries of the Gods (date unknown) Hemisphere Pictures

From Galaxies Beyond,
Travellers in Time
Leave This Prophetic Message:
WE SHALL RETURN!

They have
been here
before.
They will
come again...
SOON!

WILLIAM SHATNER'S

MYSTERIES OF THE GODS

Based on Erich von Daniken's Best-Seller of Alien Encounter

A Hemisphere Pictures Release   In Color

G | GENERAL AUDIENCES
ALL AGES ADMITTED

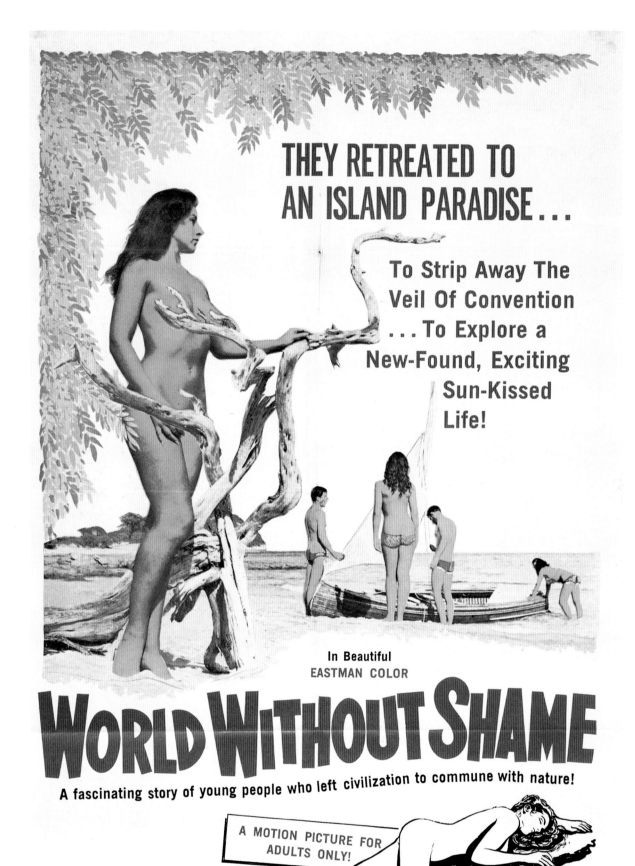

THEY RETREATED TO
AN ISLAND PARADISE...

To Strip Away The
Veil Of Convention
...To Explore a
New-Found, Exciting
Sun-Kissed
Life!

In Beautiful
EASTMAN COLOR

WORLD WITHOUT SHAME

A fascinating story of young people who left civilization to commune with nature!

A MOTION PICTURE FOR
ADULTS ONLY!

Released Thru
GALAXY FILMS, INC.

World Without Shame 1961 Galaxy
We'll Bury You! 1962 Contempora/Columbia

RED...OR DEAD!

The master plan of Communist terror that brought half the world to its knees!

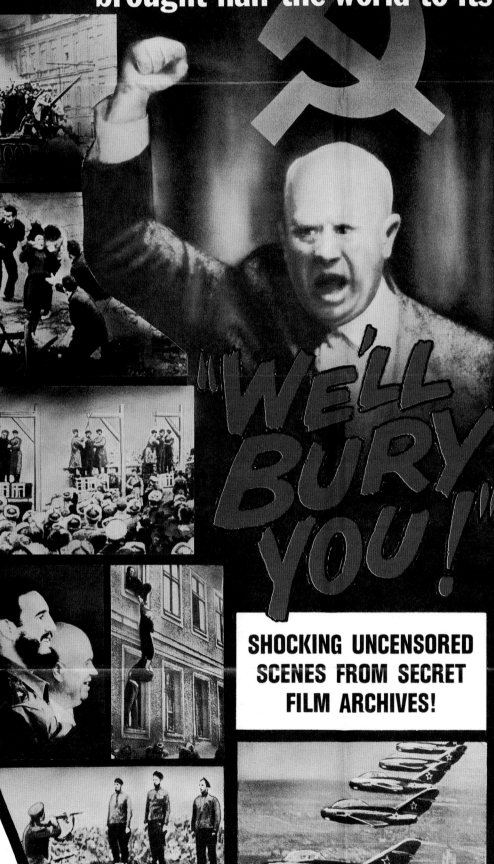

"WE'LL BURY YOU!"

SHOCKING UNCENSORED SCENES FROM SECRET FILM ARCHIVES!

SEE

THE MOST INFAMOUS CAST OF CHARACTERS EVER ASSEMBLED IN ONE FILM!

KHRUSHCHEV WORLD ENEMY #1

CASTRO BEARDED BETRAYER!

STALIN MASS-MURDERER

MAO-TSE-TSUNG RED CHINA'S TYRANT!

LENIN GENIUS OF REVOLUTION!

TROTSKY VICTIM OF REVENGE!

MALENKOV TERRORIST IN EXILE!

MIKOYAN KREMLIN'S CON-MAN

Written by JACK W. THOMAS · Produced by JACK LEEWOOD and JACK W. THOMAS · A CONTEMPORA PRODUCTION · A COLUMBIA PICTURES RELEASE

INDEX

About the Werepad
Scott Moffett and I opened the Werepad and launched our production company, Massacre at Central Hi, in 1993. With the Werepad acting as movie theater, beatnik space lounge, production facility, and home to the Cosmic Hex Archive of Xploitation film prints and movie posters—we've served up feature films, concept vinyl, and a few hundred live shows. For more dirt, visit www.werepad.com.

Jacques   Scott   Pat

Whitesploitation! 1995
Hippy Porn and A Lovely Sort of Death 2000 Massacre at Central Hi/Cosmic Hex Archive
Planet Manson 1998 Massacre at Central Hi/Cosmic Hex Archive